The Major Global Risks

Dr. Edward Schellhammer

The Major Global Risks. 1st Edition, 2017.
© Copyright. Dr. Edward Schellhammer.
All Rights Reserved.

ISBN-13: 978-1975859275
ISBN-10: 1975859278

www.EdwardSchellhammer.com
www.SchellhammerBusinessSchool.com
www.SchellhammerInstitute.com
www.SchellhammerRetreat.com

TABLE OF CONTENTS

INTRODUCTION

The Big Problems of Humanity

There are many ways to categorize the big problems of humanity. Some key words may give an idea about the complexity of the big problems of humanity:

- **Earth Population:** Increase, urban growth, youth population, elderly population
- **Poverty:** Famine, hunger, misery, lack of food and drinking water
- **Contamination:** Sewage, garbage, electro-waste, drugs, detergents, pollution, fine dust
- **Agriculture Destruction:** Drought, desertification, deforestation, flood, tornados
- **Exploitation of Manpower:** Abuse, children work, slavery, low wages, working conditions
- **Exploitation of Resources:** Food and non-food; limited water resources

- **Energy Production:** Coal, oil, gas, nuclear power stations, green energy

- **Transport:** Car traffic, public and good transport traffic (air, train, sea, bus, tram)

- **Climate Change:** Causes, effects, catastrophes and economic consequences

- **Industry:** Corporations, mass production, globalization; negative externalities

- **Economy:** Public dept, consumer dept, earnings, speculation, concentration of money

- **Banking, Monetary:** Speculation, financial crisis, money generation

- **The Rich and Superrich:** Dimensions of wealth and power

- **Extinction of Plants and Animals:** Due to contamination and climate change

- **Eco-systems:** Damages due to contamination, climate change

- **Environmental Destruction:** Due to over-construction and exploitation

- **Unemployment, Underemployment:** High rate, lack of earning (not enough work)
- **Politics:** Lack of democracy; communication, efficiency, qualifications, power abuse
- **Regulations:** Over-regulation of nearly everything, risk of police state
- **State Administration:** Quality and efficiency; the hidden dictatorship, taxes, privacy
- **Leaders and Power:** Abuse of power, world power aspiration, Illuminati, the elites
- **Military and Wars:** Militarization, wars, civil wars; terrorism; economic and cyber war
- **Trouble Spots:** Tensions, unrest, riots, civil wars, political crimes, suppression
- **Crimes:** Organized crimes, corruption; crimes, violence, cheat, scam
- **Imprisonment:** Prison life and consequences, death penalty
- **Jurisdiction:** Lack of laws for nature; power interests; police intervention

- **Physical Health:** Illnesses, accidents, health care and supply of pharmaceuticals

- **Mental Health:** Mental illnesses, behavior disorder, disease, addictions

- **Human Rights:** Disrespect, arrogance and ignorance

- **Media:** Brainwash, manipulation, misleading information, the power of the media

- **Religions:** Dogmatism, fundamentalism, superstition, deception, fabrication, lies

- **Ethics and Human Values:** Lack of moral and human values; the lost truth

- **Public Education:** Analphabetism, schizophrenic public and vocational schools

→ All these parameters are in very complex multiple interdependences.

→ All these parameters are growing with the increase of the world population

→ Humanity is in permanent connection with the collective unconscious.

→ Understanding these immense problems requires understanding history.

→ The collective unconscious contains the strongest factors of these problems.

→ It's always about humans and human factors; thus all solutions lie in humans.

→ Humans are biological, psychical (functional) and intrinsically spiritual (meaning).

→ There is only a solution for the future of humanity with the spiritual dimension.

1. RISK: WORLD POPULATION

The world population is exploding, to around 9.5 to 10 billion people by the year 2050 and by 2100: 12-14 billion.

Today there are a billion people living in absolute poverty. They live on $1 a day. Another 4-4.5 billion live in serious poverty surviving on a few Dollars to $10 per day.

Hundreds of millions of people are without work, whilst around 2 billion people have little work, or highly insecure work.

Today 50% of people live in big cities: lost, soulless, the majority breathing and drinking contaminated air and water. In the future, up to 75% will live in cities.

Famine, hunger, misery, lack of basics, food and drinking water affect up to 5 billion people.

2.6-3 billion people have no access to sanitation; sewage goes to the soil, to rivers, lakes, seas and the environment.

The sewage that goes into the sea is full of traces of medicines. When eating fish we absorb these chemicals.

The world Population growth is strongly interrelated with the global contamination.

2. RISK: NEEDS AND WANTS

Every decade more people have increasing needs and wants

In 36-45 years **an additional 3 billion people** will need food, water, health care, education, sanitation, energy, shelter, clothes, shoes, preservatives, etc.

In 36-45 years **9.5-10 billion people** will produce gigantic volumes of sewage, air pollution, chemical emissions, waste and contamination in general.

The world population growth is not just about statistics. We are talking about human beings!

Human beings have genetic codes, which determine and strive for mental and spiritual development towards optimal capacities.

Humans have 22 mental functions that need to be shaped in an appropriate way.

This correct shaping is the genuine 'Human Evolution'.

It seems:

The genuine human evolution is getting lost.

3. RISK: SCARCITY

There are today up to 6 billion people, who can't live and grow rooted in their inner mental codes. They are robots, have malformed or stunted mental functions, shaped by their environment, by mass media, mad politics, culture, wars, archaic religions, and a sad history. They are suffocated and paralyzed from endless problems throughout their lives.

Every 12-14 years an additional one billion people, **in**

total 3 billion more people in 40-45 years, will have needs and wants:

Homes, jobs, money for living, education (all levels), public health care, medicaments, sanitation, food and beverage, healthy water, electricity, gas, oil, petrol, clothes and shoes, all kinds of products, hardware, software, detergents, personal care articles, preservatives, cars and scooters, televisions, stationary articles, mobile phones, computers, internet, etc.

Result: At 10-12 billion people we need 3 planets for a sustainable life (like the average experienced in EU & USA).

4. RISK: CONTAMINATION

92% of the planet is contaminated: Waste, sewage, garbage, plastics, detergents, medicaments, drugs, nuclear and military waste. Air, soil, sea, oceans, water, nature are all contaminated.

Heavy metals can be found in animal bowels, fish and seafood.

Poisonous substances are in food, soil, air and sea.

14 billion pounds of trash is dumped in the world's oceans yearly.

250 billion of plastic pieces are swimming in the oceans; and 500m tons in the Mediterranean Sea.

223,000 barrels of nuclear waste were discharged in the North Atlantic: now leaking.

Humans, already at the fetus stage, have up to 200-350 unnatural chemicals in their body.

Nuclear waste storage must be administered for 1 million years and is a permanent risk.

Millions of tons of antibiotics are being used by humans, animal breeders and fish farms.

Hormones' substances are now found in toys, clothes and shoes.

5. RISK: ECOSYSTEMS

70 to 90% of the available water is used by agriculture and by animal breeding industries.

25-35% of all plant and animal species are at increased risk of extinction, which affects agricultural production.

About 2 billion hectares of soil have been degraded due to environmental degradation and industrialization.

Worldwide, soil erosion has caused abandonment of 4.3 million km2 of arable land during the last four decades.

Over the past 40 years, approximately 30% of the world's cropland has become unproductive.

75 billion tons of soil, the equivalent of nearly 10 million hectares of arable land, is lost every year.

By 2100 only 18 – 45% of today's rainforests will still exist. Tropical forests are home to many species.

Around 41% (other sources claim 60%) of the oceans are badly damaged as a result of human intervention.

If we destroy the ecosystems, we destroy the lives of all future generations and the genuine (Archetypal) human evolution.

6. RISK: THE HUMAN COSTS

More than 3,000,000,000 people suffer from illnesses and reduced mental capacities due to contamination.

Chemical reactions in human bodies reduce fertility, create many health problems. Hundreds of millions are affected.

Chemical contamination of the brain reduces mental capacities already during the prenatal stage: billions affected.

200-350 chemicals are in the body of fetuses, children, and adolescents, adults from toxins in breast milk, food and the environment.

Tiny doses of chemicals have a dramatic effect on the growth of a fetus: these harm the developing fetal brain.

Tiny amounts of dioxins and other toxins can damage the development of the immune and nervous systems.

Nobody knows how the human body of billions will react above a certain level of these toxic cocktails.

7. RISK: CLIMATE CHANGE

Carbon dioxide, methane and nitrogen oxides are the gases that produce global warming.

Global emission of carbon dioxide will increase until 2030 by 40%.

Acidification of the oceans is a major threat to marine life and humanity's food supply.

The melting of Arctic and Antarctic ice started 1990. Glaciers are now melting twice as fast as in 1999.

Today every year more ice is melting than the amount of ice that exists in the Alps.

The global average sea level will probably rise by 60 cm or 1 meter and higher by the end of the century. Many islands and coastal towns will be lost at a global warming of 2ºC, already reached in 2016. Since the start of the 21st century the level has already risen by 20-30 centimeters.

The average global warming will reach 4º in the year 2100 with disastrous effects.

8. RISK: WEATHER EFFECTS

More than 135 cities near coastlines will be heavily affected if not entirely destroyed.

Areas of land vulnerable to flooding will increase by about 50% in the next 40 years.

As a result of the ice melting the algal bloom in the Arctic comes earlier; with major consequences for the food chain.

Widespread flooding as a result of an increase in sea levels will create major upheaval for hundreds of millions of people. Most coastline land will be heavily affected.

General: Heat waves, droughts, fires, rainstorms, floods, tornados, hurricanes, and tropical cyclones.

Mediterranean and other subtropical regions: increase in wildfires and tropical storms.

Frequent droughts and higher global temperatures could destroy by 2100 up to 70% of the Amazon rain forest.

Huge parts of the planet, beset with over-population, droughts, soil erosion, freak storms, massive crop failures and rising sea levels, will be unfit for human existence.

9. RISK: FUTURE PERSPECTIVES

3.2-4 billion people will experience water shortages due to Climate Change.

Water shortages (2015: 40% already lost) and hunger will be an ever-growing threat.

Every year an average of over 400 million people are directly exposed to a flood.

Climate Change and its consequences will produce inter-regional migration of peoples of unknown dimensions.

200-500 million are to be displaced due to rising sea levels, heavier floods, and more intense droughts.

Floods will affect 2 billion by 2050 due to climate change, deforestation, rising sea levels, more migrations.

An additional 600 million people are at risk of famine due to climate change.

Most of the world's major river deltas are sinking, increasing the flood risk faced by hundreds of millions of people.

Climate Change will result in a global catastrophe costing millions of lives in chaos, wars and natural disasters.

10. RISK: ECONOMY

3.5 billion People live on less than $2.50 per day.
5.6 billion People live on less than $10 per day.
The remaining 1.4bn population is much better off.

1826 billionaires (2015) with aggregate net worth of $7.05 trillion.

The global financial elite dispose of $42.7 trillion.

2016: 62 people have as much wealth as worlds' 3.7bn poorest people.

The Superrich: Concentration of wealth versus 5.4bn poor people.

Banking, Monetary: Speculation, financial crisis, money creation, cheating, scamming, abuse, no transparency.

Economy: Public debt, consumer debt, low earnings, reduced living standard, unemployment, concentration of wealth, no transparency.

Over the past 50 years 60% of the global ecosystems have been irreparably damaged for the sake of highest possible profit for a few mad people.

All future generations for millenniums to come will have to live the consequences.

11. RISK: EXPLOITATION

Exploitation of Manpower: Child labor, slavery, low wages, miserable working conditions.

Arable land: soil degradation (over-exploitation, chemicals).

Extreme exploitation of resources, sea-fruit, fishes, water resources, forests, and so on.

Negative externalities of mining (toxins, poisoned land, water); victims: people, land, water.

Most natural resources much overexploited; destroyed in 40 years.

Wheat, grain, corn, rice, cocoa, fruit juices, , meat, sugar, coffee are fields for speculators.

200 years for future generations to pay for 152 trillion public debts.

200 years for future generations to pay for the public finance losses.

300-500 or more years for future generations to pay for the destroyed planet.

Technological innovations will replace 75% of all work.

Technology will radically dominate the global market. High global unemployment, followed by poverty, will globally be the standard.

12. RISK: WAYS OF LIVING

'Deicide': Killing God. Humans can't kill the Creator.

Therefore, they kill his creations, in the end the elimination of human evolution.

'Deicide' means: Hate for life and for the creation, in action: destroying the planet with all its ecosystems, humans, humans' potentials, folks, nations, societies, cultures, peace on earth, justice, healthy food and drinking water.

Deicide is a globally operating virus. The virus has infected societies, people, the planet. The virus creates imbalance in society and in the mind of people.

The virus creates strife, animosity, distrust, and hostility everywhere.

The virus loves wars and the most atrocious criminals have always been politicians and the rulers of the monetary systems.

In 10-15 years around 95% of the global ecosystems humans depend on will be damaged.

80% of the world population must expect serious consequences in 20-30 years.

13. RISK: POLITICS

Politics ignores most precious human values many pioneers identified over centuries and millenniums.

Politics is cynical, hostile, arrogant, and bellicose towards the people, provinces and other nations.

Politics is not connected with the people, the sovereignty of people, and the lives of the people.

Political democratic practices and declarations are a ridiculous masquerade of gigantic scams.

Politics is a world of incompetence and extreme lack

of understanding of people and their lives.

A systemic anti-evolutionary virus is present in all the halls, lobbies, foyers and anterooms of power; wheeling, dealing and manipulating like puppet masters behind the curtains.

Politics is the worst possible nest of a perverse super-narcissism, which always needs an enemy to rectify their exploitative existence and warmongering.

14. RISK: HISTORY OF WARS

14,500 wars during the last 5,000 years!
Since 1945 wars staged by United States and NATO without being attacked or in danger.
1945-2012: Estimated 270 wars plus estimated 130 war-like conflicts involving US and NATO.
US and NATO killed millions, destroyed entire countries, created immeasurable misery and

suffering.

Christianity has killed through wars 'in the Name of God and Jesus Christ' up to 1bn people.

Staged American and NATO (proxy) wars without being attacked:

Vietnam (1964-1975)

Grenada (1983)

Panama (1989)

Iraq/Golf War I, II (1991)

Somalia (1993)

Bosnia (1992-1995)

Yugoslavia (1999)

Afganistán (2001-2016)

Iraq (2003)

Venezuela, Ecuador (2008)

Tunisia, Libya (2011)

Syria, Lebanon (2011-2015)

Yemen, Iraq (2015)

Ukraine Civil War (2014-2015)

Nuclear weapons and other weapons of mass destruction are the most evil invention in the history of humanity!

15. RISK: POLITICIANS AND PEOPLE

Most politicians have no comprehensive knowledge of the peoples' situation, of humanity, the planet. Most politicians have an archaic understanding of mankind - in the core unchanged since millenniums.

Politicians have always acted with megalomania, greed, arrogance, falseness, scrupulousness, and amorality.

People suffer from the abuse of political power, from lies and incompetence in governments.

People are exploited as human biomass by industry,

economies, politics, banks, and military.

People cannot even enjoy a condom or a chewing gum without paying some cents to the tax man.

People will have to pay interest of repayments on exorbitant public debt and costs of wars for generations.

Police state and full of control of all people is already implemented.

A majority of governments are destroying the livelihoods of their future generations.

16. RISK: PUBLIC EDUCATION

Failures are:

1) The ignorance and exclusion of human's spiritual intelligence, emotional intelligence, intuition and

creativity.

2) The lack of education for mastering life: money-, self- and life management, relationships, marriage, family life, etc.

3) The ignorance about human values such as love, care, truth, psycho-social security, inner roots of integrity (ethics).

4) The lack of complex thinking about life, spirituality, mind, environment, politics, media, consumption.

5) The absence of topics such as lies, cheating, deceit, falseness, narcissism, neurotics, psychopaths, brainwash.

6) The absence of spiritual needs, understanding meaning, dealing with dreams, and psychical-spiritual development.

7) Public education is still based on a concept of mankind, which is rooted in an archaic and highly undeveloped mind.

17. RISK: MASS MEDIA

People copy inefficient and illusionary patterns of solutions for all kind of concerns.

People copy the kind of communication and behavior they see in the media.

There is absolutely no psychical-spiritual support transmitted from the media.

TV shapes the mind, idealizes soulless humans, and makes people stupid or helpless. TV consumers are not just brainwashed, but, entirely dehumanized.

People are brainwashed with an illusionary world, an

impossible self-identity.

Most marketing of corporate groups destroys the inner life and authentic natural growth of people.

In TV programs, there are no or rarely genuine human values that shape true human evolution.

Mass Media is destroying human evolution, creating dehumanization, crushing all precious human values, and therefore are highly responsible for the dire global state of humanity.

18. RISK: ACCREDITATION

Accreditation criteria are based on totalitarian, compulsive control of every tinny element.

Accredited degree programs serve ultimately the power interests of the top elites.

Accredited degree programs have no chance to critically respond to the world.

Accreditation criteria don't allow investigating the lies of Western (and Eastern) politics and history.

Accreditation criteria don't allow investigating the perverse propaganda concepts.

Accredited degree programs castrate the potentials and talents of the teachers.

Accreditation is anti-evolutionary, anti-truth, anti-democratic, anti-free market, a scam.

Public Education is founded on an archaic understanding of humans and human life, not on human evolution.

Public Education does not consider a holistic forming of the mental functions and the meaning of being a human.

19. RISK: RELIGION

Teaching excludes the holistic shaping of the mind; worse: has no concept of psychical-spiritual development.

Religions have forgotten the eternal Archetypes of the Soul, which are indispensable in order to reach complete fulfillment.

Archaic religions abuse the laziness, narrow mental qualities, high greed, and fearfulness of the people.

Religion, its teaching and practices, can't be better than the operational quality of the shaped mental functions of their agents, authorities and naïve believers.

All stories in the Old and New Testament are

legends, myths, sagas, fictions, anecdotes, full of manipulation and deceit.

Primary texts of Holy Scriptures don't exist.

The Old Testament is an artifact with many erratic statements from different societies over millenniums.

Religions have stolen the transcendental archetypal experiences that wise people, spiritual kings, and prophets performed and received in dreams.

20. RISK: DELUSIONS

The word 'Spirituality' has been distorted, abused, filled with hot air billions of times.

Spiritual qualities require the efficient functioning of all mental functions.

The spiritual intelligence is creating the dreams in order to guide humans towards completeness and fulfillment.

The spiritual intelligence is the only source to understand soul and God (dreams).
Dreams can't be manipulated.

Humans want easy, fast, simple and direct solutions for their salvation.

Humans do not want to take responsibility for the truth and their holistic development.

Humans themselves play false, mendacious and deceitful games in life.

Humans don't have substantial knowledge to question themselves let alone others.

Humans believe in archaic nonsense because they

themselves are archaic and live non-sense.

21. RISK: GENUINE ROOTS OF RELIGION

Nothing is authentically documented about Abraham, Moses, Jesus, Apostles, and Gospels. Nothing in the Bible is 'holy'. Religions are never 'infallible'.

In the history of mankind, the inner Spirit in the soul of some wise men and women made vivid these Archetypes in their mind and soul.

We do not have any authentic proof of the inner processes of any Prophet, documented with dreams and practical work.

Human being, love, joy, zest for life, peace, satisfaction, happiness, hope, justice, the inner Spirit, balance, aim, completeness, totality, openness, confidence, psychical-spiritual evolution, fulfillment, conjunction of the real and spiritual world, source of life, renewal, reconciliation, salvation, forgiveness, and presence of God.

Leaders and agents of Religions today do not know anything substantial about the archetypal processes of the soul all genuine prophets had to go through.

22. RISK: INTERRELATIONS

- Each complex parameter has a dynamic of its own.
- The mega-parameters build up accumulation.
- Accumulation occurs over decades and centuries.
- There is a rapid increase zof accumulation in all fields.

- There are complex interrelations between systems.

- All parameters stay in interdependences of others.

- All systems show all-embracing negative effects.

- There are interactions between systems and humans.

- The complex dynamics have no boundaries.

- Criticalities are bounded in systemic conditions.

- Ideological and dogmatic belief increases criticalities.

- Humans are always the responsible agents.

- The roots of evil lie in the malformed minds of people.

- In all systems, we identify systematic dehumanization.

- There is systemic hate for God and the creation everywhere.

- The dynamic of all parameters is coded for Deicide.

All criticalities of humanity and the planet are accumulating and increasing exponentially.

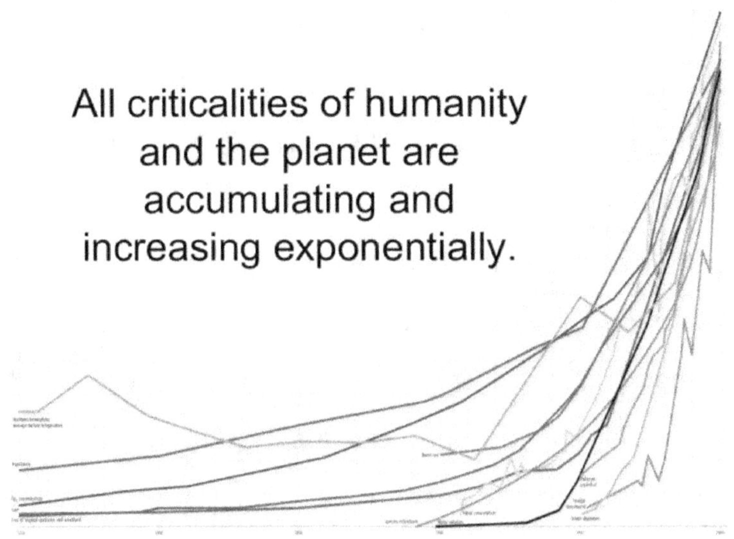

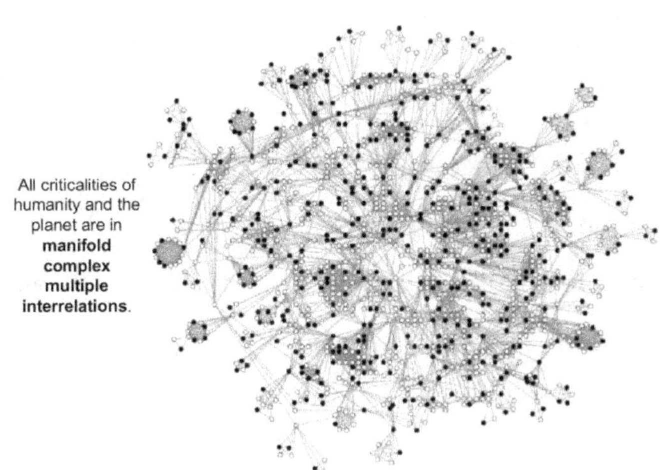

All criticalities of
humanity and the
planet are in
**manifold
complex
multiple
interrelations**.

23. RISK: FUTURE DEVELOPMENT

People have made terrible mistakes; but they can profoundly learn from them.

People have ignored and neglected the most important human values.

People have lost themselves in running after illusions, and for superficial or egoistic purposes.

People have played with lies, cheat, deceit, distortion, delusion and empty promises.

People have ignored that all humans on earth are a divine creation.

There are no solutions:

1. In archaic concepts of humanity.
2. In fundamentalist ideologies and dogmas.
3. In disrespecting humans' genuine inner and terrestrial needs.
4. In violence, ignorance, arrogance, hubris and cynicism.

5. In delusions, everywhere. People don't want the truth.

There is no solution without the Archetypes of the Soul, the principles of genuine human evolution, which are related to the development of all mental functions.

24. RISK: CHANGES AND RENEWAL

People must change their view, thinking, attitudes, and ways of living.

☑ People must find new faith in themselves, in their inner Spirit, in their inner potentials.

☑ People must become creative, innovative and pioneering for new knowledge and new solutions.

☑ People must aspire to new goals and meaning of life with strength, endurance and perseverance.

☑ People must cooperate, talk, discuss without taboos and take decisions together.

☑ People must go through a catharsis and complete renewal for the future generations.

☑ People must solve the immense global problems with soul and mind, but not with wars.

☑ People must unify humanity for a cooperative, balanced, peaceful and equitable path of genuine evolution.

Holistic and permanent all-embracing psychical-spiritual development aiming for inner satisfaction and fulfillment must become subjects and topics of science and public education adapted by all education levels.

25. THE 25 GLOBAL RISKS

Killing God by Destroying the Planet and Humanity is called: "Deicide".

Global Threat 1: Admiration of the Evil

- The social belonging and acceptance of everything that is extreme, bad and evil.
- The promotion of everyone that is brutal, inconsiderate and strong.
- The immediate social exclusion of everyone that is critical and on alert.
- The exposure of the masses to brutal violence and gore in films and TV series.
- The abuse of children via sexualized marketing.
- The glorification of loud, vulgar, obscene, aggressive and stupid characters on TV.
- The environment of Western societies is not made for children.

- 90% of what TV-channels offer is intentionally for dehumanization.
- Most big social networking websites promote self-alienation and narcissism.
- The use of the word 'marriage' for homosexuals destroys its archetype.
- The neo-capitalistic axis of evil is destroying societies and their values.
- The absence of love shows the disconnection from the source of life.
- The 'third age group' is extremely separated from the younger generations.

Global Threat 2: Falseness

- The abused, exploited and truly hollow values of "democracy".
- The false and evil "tolerance" that pushes for "anything goes" to sow discord.
- The sports industry is soulless and promotes only the ideal of 'the best'.

- The promotion of solutions that neglect and hide the source of problems.
- The inhuman and false understanding of crime as criminal versus social product.
- The evil scientific pursuit of "out surviving" problems versus "source solutions".
- The hysterical victimization of false players and evil doers.
- The heroic presentation and promotion of artists who are merely talent less freaks.
- The polarization of every topic that has led to a complete lack of discourse.
- The falseness executed in the name of "humanitarian aid" and "social programs".
- The pure evil behind the alibi of philanthropy and donations.

Global Threat 3: Corporations

- The sole interest in the elderly generation is the economic factor.

- The unknown risk of genetic modification disrespects the creation.
- The negative externalities of the industry are an expression of deicide.
- The tastelessness of fruit and vegetables, grown to norms and standards.
- The destructive development towards "corporate" in every industry/sector.
- The falsenesses of fining corporations for destruction, offences and crimes.
- The extreme concentration of money and thus effectively power.
- The soulless economy that led to the definition of value solely through wealth.
- The desperate dependence on technology for everyday survival.
- The risks of nuclear power stations show the cynicism of its advocacy.
- The future risks and costs of nuclear waste express hate for humanity.

<u>Global Threat 4: Politics</u>

- Men older than 48 are required a lot less in the professional world (work).
- Women older than 43 are required a lot less in the professional world (work).
- People above the age 52-55 have a significantly low chance of finding a job.
- Politics, economy, and religion sow distrust in all social constellations.
- Wages (full time jobs) that do not allow for a modest living express hate.
- The agents of CIA, MI5 and Mossad that operate for the deicide.
- The foundation of Israel (1948) is a declaration of war against God.
- Tax systems in the Western world have degraded humans to slaves.
- The over-regulations everywhere have killed the dynamic of evolution.

- The admiration of struggle versus mediation, clashes versus understanding.

Global Threat 5: Warmongers

- Those who started building nuclear bombs were Satan's servants.
- Those who permanently rearm and force others to follow destroy God.
- All wars of the Western coalition since 1946 express hate for human life.
- The most sophisticated weapons developed from US-NATO, the weapon industry
- The jurisdiction in America and Europe protecting the supreme masters of deicide
- The jurisdiction protecting the increasing destruction of all Archetypes of the Soul

Global Threat 6: Subrogation

- The people are helpless.

- The people are ensnared.

- The people are lied to.

- The people are brainwashed.

- The people need to be blind.

- The people should shut up.

- The people should not think.

- The people cannot have a soul.

- The people should not ask questions.

- The people should see lies as the truth.

- The people should see neurosis as something healthy.

- The people should see lunacy as a mission.

- The people should experience narcissism as wellbeing.

- The people should go to the doctor.

- The people should go to the pharmacy.

- The people should be (relatively) poor.

- The people should suffer from emissions.

- The people must suffer in general.

Global Threat 7: Enslavement

- The people should consume.

- The people should feel lust when shopping.

- The people are chained to credit.

- The people are allowed to buy a car.

- The people should use credit cards.

- The people are allowed to have a cell phone.

- The people should lose themselves on the Internet.

- The people are allowed to have fun.

- The people can speculate.

- The people can have a swimming pool.

- The people can have a walkway.

- The people can go on holiday.

- The people should get meaningless things cheap.

- The people who are critical need to go into psychotherapy.

- The people who do not follow the lunacy must be punished.

Global Threat 8: Humans and Malformed Creation

- Humans are lazy, lazy to think, sluggish, superficial, don't want to learn.
- Humans want easy, fast, simple and direct solutions for their salvation.
- Humans are submissive to authority, easily deceivable and easily enslaved.
- Humans are like blind sheep, driven herd animals and followers.
- Human are cowardly and fearfully paralyzed by social pressure.
- Humans want to belong, otherwise they are alone and excluded.
- Humans themselves play a false, deceitful, deceiving game in life.
- Humans are psychically on the stage of development of a small child.
- Humans have enormous concealed guilt, partly real and partly self suggested.
- Humans do not have any substantial self enlightenment and do not want any.

- Humans do not want to see, how their own parents are completely archaic.
- Humans are scared, to look at themselves in the inner mirror.
- Humans believe in 'holy lies' because they themselves lie, live in lies.
- Humans believe in archaic nonsense, because they themselves are archaic.

Global Threat 9: Humans and Belief as Compensation

- Humans need the belief in order to live their quarrelsomeness.
- Humans cannot give up their belief, because they are stubborn.
- Humans live their sick cantankerousness with their belief.
- Humans are scared of life and therefore cling to their belief.
- Humans can live their own, open or concealed arrogance with their belief.

- Humans have such a small ego, that they refurbish it with belief.
- Humans think they are better with their belief, than non-believers.
- Humans compensate their weak, instable self-confidence with their belief.
- Humans flee from themselves and their own inferiority with their belief.
- Humans see their life as unworthy and low; create balance with belief.
- Humans cannot live themselves and need the 'mother church'.
- Humans increase their extremely low and bad self value with their belief.
- Humans tame with belief their 'unworthy' compulsiveness and lust.

Global Threat 10: Belief for Displacement

- Humans hope for the redemption of their unconscious complexes with belief.

- Humans compensate their human weaknesses with their belief.
- Humans expect help from God and J.C. instead of helping themselves.
- Humans conceal with their low psychical-spiritual development with their belief.
- Humans have not been loved and hope to receive the love of God with their belief.
- Humans suppress their hate of their father, mother and life with their belief.
- Humans have an increased feeling of triumph, being in the "true" belief.
- Humans strengthen their own imperiousness and their tyrannical personality.
- Humans choose illusions over the strong facts of life and human being.
- Humans have experienced suffering and in their belief experience comfort and relief.
- Humans don't have a genuine self-identity and find it in their community of believers.

- Humans are sickened by themselves, their own body and flee into belief.

Global Threat 11: Humans and Fear of the Truth

- Humans are scared of the shock that the truth can release.
- Humans do not want to take responsibility for the truth.
- Humans do not have any substantial knowledge, to question themselves or others.
- Humans are submissive and masochistically bonded in their drive to religion.
- Humans are orally unsaved and nurture themselves through fixation on belief.
- Humans are scared, to recognize the devilish lies of the church.
- Humans fear to recognize themselves, how they are deceived by the religion.
- Humans lose their ground, when they recognize 'infallible' truth as a lie.

→ These are the best conditions to mentally subjugate humans.

→ Religious subjugation serves the politics and the economics.

Global Threat 12: Failure of Public Education

- The ignorance and exclusion of human's spiritual intelligence, emotional intelligence, intuition and creativity
- The lack of education for mastering life: money, self- and life management, relationship, marriage, family life, etc.
- The ignorance about human values such as love, care, truth, psycho-social security, inner roots of integrity (ethics)
- The lack of complex thinking about life philosophy, spirituality, mind, environment, politics, media, consumption

- The absence of topics such as lies, cheat, deceit, falseness, narcissism, neurotics, psychopaths, brainwash, etc.

Global Threat 13: Absence of Evolution

- The disrespect for individual differences such as personality, character, performance, talents, inner potentials
- The performance criteria that ignore practical relevance, human values and a holistic humane education
- The lack of joyful learning, creative learning activities, respect for the psychical-spiritual process of learning
- The lack of promotion of self-confidence, critical explorations of the world, respect for 'being a human on earth'
- The lack of promoting the genuine inner needs for working as a part of satisfaction, fulfillment and meaning of life

- The lack of pioneering spirit due to rigidity of fully standardized curriculums (e.g. businesses, social sciences) and the boring practical trainings

Global Threat 14: Failure of Authorities in Education

- The paralyzing of teacher's creativity and inner dedication due to prescribed dominant intellectual curriculums
- The inability to rapidly respond to new educational needs related to fast changes in society and the world
- The constrained and obsessive accreditations (standardizations) of public education (including social sciences such as economics and business in general)
- The centralization of public education with a highly rigid innovative inflexibility of institutions and curriculums

- The incompetent and immature politicians and experts in the local and national departments of education

- The ideological interests that shaped curriculums, exam practices, principles of selection, school career and professional career

- The rigid, arrogant and authoritarian atmosphere towards children and adolescents in educational institutions

Global Threat 15: Dehumanization

- Billions of people have no knowledge, skills or methods to understand themselves and their life, their difficulties, their problems and conflicts.

- Billions of people are brainwashed, manipulated, suppressed and infiltrated by lies, cheat, fictions, illusions, seductions, false games, and a perverse and neurotic collective theater.

- Billions of people want to love and to be loved, want happiness and satisfaction, success and a secure life environment. But they all have no idea how to achieve such life aims.

• Billions of people are pushed into a mental and emotional chaos, into stress and fear, into countless meanders, into endless problems and conflicts without a chance to evade.

• Billions of people are treated like pure human biomass, partly lured with money and partly terrorized by poverty and misery. Nobody gives them hope and solutions.

Global Threat 16: Failures: Religions. State Schools. Politics. Education.

• Billions of people suffer from frightening collective failure. They all have questions about life, love, relationships, spirituality, sexuality, dreams, emotions, feelings and problems.

• They need knowledge, skills, guidance and support to understand themselves, their life, and to master life for the fulfillment of their longing.

- All humans have dreams. Dreams give important messages. But billions can't interpret their dreams. They can't benefit from this spiritual power that gives guidance and support.

- Education about psychical-spiritual development is fundamental for the youth and for all adults, including about new ways of living and understanding of man and human life.

- Further education is also strongly recommended for self-employed people and small businesses, including advanced business knowledge.

- Further education is indispensable for all people in responsible positions in politics, media, economy, industry, education, religion, etc.

The lies replaced the truth. Every soul is abused and violated.

Global Threat 17: The Educational Authorities

- Express old-fashioned political egomania: 'now I have the say, I have control'
- Totalitarian, arrogant and mad control of absolutely everything
- Extreme psychopathological, all-round compulsive control
- Regulative rules that suffocate any progressive pioneering innovations
- Full of straitjackets that paralyze any creative development
- A dictatorial concept that forces all cultural identities on a global level
- Megalomaniac entitlements driven by psychotic beliefs
- Blindly and radically obsessed with sticking their nose into everything
- Arrogant intrusion into alien and foreign educational affairs
- Obsessed with brainwashing mankind already from an early childhood

- Authorities are pure parasites and exploiters of internal business 'secrets'
- Authorities are as a whole Necrophiliac, anti-spiritual, programmed for deicide

Global Threat 18: Systemic Control of Education

- An archaic understanding (concept) of mankind and society
- Basically a 'copy and paste'- education: memorizing and exams
- Perverse obstruction of all mental, psychical and spiritual potentials
- Strong expressions of meddling, brainwashing and manipulation
- Conceitedness in their 'superior' race, social 'way of life', and scientific knowledge
- Not proven, but probable and possible abuse of very private information
- Promote cantankerousness, neurotic patterns, and extreme rigidity in social behavior

- Confusing labyrinth of norms, rules, and regulations around every 'corner'
- Sap and undermine the authority (head, director) of educational institutions
- Make educational institutions dependent, submissive, and obedient
- A fully rational and mechanistic approach excluding capacities of organism
- Are capable of destroying by simply rejecting a renewal of accreditation
- Outrageously strive to devalue educational authorities and institutions
- Destroy unique 'peculiarities' of societies, ways of living and understanding of life
- Are driven by an insane 'mission' that can only lead to the destruction of humanity

Global Threat 19: Lack of Knowledge and Skills

- Learning, studying attitudes
- In touch with nature

- Attitude for working daily

- Sustainable decision making

- Attitude for lifelong working

- Understanding the world

- Understanding politics

- Understanding society

- Skills for mastering life

- Critical view over religions

- Communication skills

- Critical view over ideologies

- Reading to understand

- Critical about media content

- Care for environment/nature

- Skills to manage people

- Skills to manage peace

- Clear, complex perception

- Knowing the spiritual source

- Precise, analytical thinking

- Picture: past-present-future

- Interpreting one's dreams

- Skills for family life

- Exploring the unconscious

- Conscious way of living

- Care for baby/child/teenager

- Ready for global renewal

- Generally critical, vigilant

- Free from brainwashing

- Physical health sustainability

- Inner male-female balance

- Mental health sustainability

- Meditating to understand

Global Threat 20: Absence of Personal Development

- Moral character, Integrity

- Knowledge about inner life

- Ability to love and care

- Reliable and trustworthy

- Living human values

- Living inner potentials

- Holistic personal growth

- Using spiritual intelligence

- Authentic being and living

- Systematic self-knowledge

- Free of compensatory behavior

- Achieved inner fulfillment

- Pioneering, vanguard spirit

- Humble, decent, responsible

- Sexual satisfaction

- To stand for the truth

- Sustainable personal lifestyle

- Fulfilled personal catharsis

- Inner archetypal experiences

Is there a Solution for Humanity?

YES!

THE FOUNDER

Dr. Edward Schellhammer is the founder and President of the Schellhammer Education Group that includes the Schellhammer Business School, the Schellhammer Institute and the Schellhammer Retreat.

What is most striking about meeting Dr. Edward Schellhammer beyond his pleasant and polite manner; youthful disposition or passionate and sincere views on humanity and the planet, is his unshakable conviction that the world needs a new pioneering education.

But exactly who is Dr. Edward Schellhammer? Is he a Philosopher, an expert on human matters, a Psychologist, a prolific author of over 30 titles from psychology to politics and economics, an educator, or a visionary with a profound and beneficial insight into the human condition?

The answer is that he is all that and more. In different age, he would have been called a polymath, and probably kept close company with those giants of The Age of Enlightenment, like his fellow countryman Jean Jacques Rousseau, Thomas Payne and perhaps even Thomas Jefferson. For, it is exactly this gift of enlightenment that Dr. Schellhammer wants to give humanity.

He reveals: "My studies, global travels, professional experiences and extensive study and research since 1970 have given me a clear and unique insight into humanity, human evolution, spirituality, education, cultures, needs, values, standards and our purpose in life like no other!"

Pausing to add: "Humanity hasn't even begun to discover what the true path of human life on earth is fundamentally good and right for".

Born and educated in Switzerland he has lived in

Paris, South of France, London, Kiel, Detroit, and Mexico, before settling in Marbella, Spain, some 27 years ago.

He studied Education, Psychology, Psychoanalysis, and Philosophy. He was a lecturer at the University of Zurich as well as other institutions, and as a member of international workshops he dedicated his ample energy to futurology, future perspectives of humanity, peace and disarmament, development of education in Latin America and key global issues in general, concentrating on developing a new understanding of politics and economics for the future. His findings are indispensable for all those who value life, love, and justice.

He places great emphasis on Dream Theory a subject that he has researched for most of his life and passionately believes in, declaring that some 35 years ago he had a dream that told him to solve the mystery of man and human evolution. Stating categorically: "My initial reaction was, this is an impossible task!" and then quickly adds with equal conviction: "But today, I think, no, I know, that I have discovered all the fundamental components that explain the mystery of man and human evolution."

With his professional background, he has written many books spanning: Individuation (holistic personal development), Dream Theory and Interpretation, Problem Solving, The Individual and Collective Unconscious, Love and Relationships, The Archetypes of Man, The Future of Humanity, Global Human Education, New Philosophical Anthropology, Didactics in Teaching and Counseling and Coaching.

All inner processes – psychical, spiritual and practical – to find and live the (archetypal) codes of human evolution are well documented like never before in the history of mankind. Everything that you need to learn is elaborated in his books.

Dr. Edward Schellhammer has unveiled the mystery of mankind, the psychological-spiritual and archetypal codes of human evolution. It has taken 35 years to understand humans, the divine and factual human evolution, the mendacious aims of politics, economy, public education, religion, spirituality, and the state of humanity and the world, in order to offer you today the eternally valid concept (codes) of the Archetypal Human Evolution.

During the last 35 years he had around 14,000 dreams about the state and development of humanity, the world and the planet. Countless dreams have shown him everything of fundamental relevance for humanity's future and evolution.

During the same period, he also had estimated 3,000 dreams about the genuine archetypal evolution of mankind, the state and potentials of the mind and of the world population, the 'other world' and God. He has been in his dreams in the 'other world', in the divine paradise, and he has experienced the 'Union with God' as well as many more archetypal processes. He profoundly elaborated all this; estimated 80,000 hours of explorations and analysis in total.

Dr. Edward Schellhammer says: "The never achieved most advanced psychological, spiritual, archetypal, educational and practical concept, the Philosophical Anthropology of the Archetypal Human Evolution, is prepared and can lead humanity to hope, peace, justice, balance, truthfulness, and fulfillment."

Like the man himself his books are not for the faint hearted with challenging, pioneering and vanguard content and new ways of thinking that covers shaping of the mind, personal development, human values, human evolution, life, business, politics, economy, society, education, and religion – for everybody that is searching for the truth and for a fundamental personal fulfillment. Reading his books is pure adventure for the mind.

After decades of extensive explorations, research, analysis, writing and sometimes personal retreat, Dr. Edward Schellhammer is now at the disposal of discerning individuals and institutions wishing to pursue prepared and tailor-made programs of evolutionary further education.

HUMANITY NEEDS A NEW CONCEPT FOR 'MANKIND', A NEW SPIRITUALITY, AND A NEW BREED OF EVOLUTIONARY HUMANS!

HUMANITY NEEDS A NEW GENERATION OF ALL-ROUND PREPARED LEADERS IN EVERY FIELD OF HUMAN ENDEAVOR!

HUMANITY NEEDS A NEW CONCEPT OF BUSINESS SCHOOLS, OF UNIVERSITIES, AND OF A NEW PUBLIC EDUCATION!

HUMANITY NEEDS TO RECLAIM THE ARCHETYPAL SPIRITUALITY ('RELIGION') THAT WAS NEVER ESTABLISHED IN THE PAST!

17.04.2011 I dreamt: "The door to Paradise must now be completely closed for all souls, until the complete enlightenment of the truth is fulfilled globally." Therefore, with all the power of attorney from my spiritual (archetypal) authority [that has given it to me in dreams] and in order to save the human evolution I decide today:

I will not let a single soul into Paradise, apart from a few exceptions, until the deicide octopus is detected and disclosed, until the truth is researched and clarified and put on the table, and until both are fully understood by the entire humanity. Everyone is summoned to work on this catharsis and renewal: Researchers, experts, scientists, journalists, politicians, legal professionals, CEOs, and all varieties of power holders and religious officials; but also, all and every single citizen of all states and nations.

"As the highest judge of all souls living in the other world and of all souls living today and in the future on this earth, I will severely punish the supreme masters of deicide with a minimum of 50,000 years being far away from God and his light, the protagonists with a minimum of 10,000 years, and all other significant collaborators of deicide will not see God and his light for a very long time. People that are unwilling to learn and to develop themselves psychically and spiritually and those who infect the collective (entire societies) with brainwashing, lies and falseness, with their insane narcissism, perverse neurosis, psychosis, psychopathy and madness cannot expect to be allowed to enter into paradise. It is said since millenniums: If a folk and its government ignore its new (genuine, provable) prophet, destroy his life, bans him, and paralyzes with that his divine mission for humanity and the archetypal human evolution, this folk will lose its land. Switzerland is already sentenced. The same punishment is applied for any folk that acts in the same way against this prophet for humanity in the third Millennium. If all of humanity accepts the deicide simply by ignoring it, then most souls will be sent for 200,000 years to a dark place far away from the paradise of God."

THE FOUNDATION FOR A NEW PATH

THE MANIFESTO (ISBN: 1494855917): The book unveils the state of people, of humanity, of the world and the planet. People destroy the evolution of humanity with their blinded religious, atheist or other mental or political insanity. The Manifesto puts the challenge on the table, as never before! Not wanting to know is a shame. How can you be happy with a suppressed shame? You can only become free inside with knowledge, critical thinking, and self-contemplation. This book tells you the 'truth' about the world and the lost archetypal path of humanity!

ARMAGEDDON OR EVOLUTION (ISBN: 1484868668): There are only two options: Humanity's leaders take responsibility to manage evolution in a sustainable manner, or the systemic fissures will crush mankind and the planet will degenerate. The book reveals how everybody can contribute to a sustainable human life. Why should you have a good life if you don't contribute for a better world? The book contains all you need to know about the species called 'human': fulfilling ways of living, evolutionary personality development, man-woman-relationship aiming for 'completeness', a substantial advanced philosophy about humans, and a realistic overview of the big problems around the globe.

THE FUTURE IN YOUR HANDS (ISBN: 1478377917): The truths and facts are outrageous and beyond all imagination. The damages worldwide are monstrous. Everybody pays with their taxes during centuries for ignoring the ongoing massive destruction and wars. Nevertheless, everybody can contribute to create a new path for humanity. The state of humanity and the world - preprogrammed from previous generations - shows us that most parents don't care about what the future will bring to their children. If parents don't care about the future of their children, then the young generation must learn to take their future into their own hands!

DEICIDE (ISBN: 1478366524): Indicted: The supreme masters of neo-capitalism, the leaders of corporations, banks, politics, media, justice, the ultra-high net worth individuals, the leaders of education, universities, Christianity; humans that destroy the genuine human values and that accept the lies as the truth. Those who seriously want to understand the mess also get the conceptual solutions. A must read for all those who work in the education sector, in politics, economy or religion.

BECOME A STRONG PERSONALITY (ISBN: 1478372958): The book provides everything that all people must develop for a sustainable inner foundation in order to be prepared for a fast-changing world. It is ridiculous and stupid if you do not want to become a genuine, strong personality. Read this to prepare yourself for the world!

LOVE YOUR LIFE (ISBN: 1478372834): Everybody needs to build up the ability to love, and to live joy of life. The book provides everything that must be developed in order to find happiness. Most people do not have the slightest idea what love is about. It's much more than an emotion. A must for anyone interested in genuine love!

60 DAYS TO PARADISE (ISBN: 1480177369): Everybody needs to learn about how to develop a better life. The book provides countless tips and practical suggestions to reach genuine success. The paradise is within you. Therefore: Do you want darkness and the hell inside or the eternal sun? You will find out how to create your inner sun.

PRACTICAL PSYCHOLOGY (ISBN: 147836694X): The book provides immense knowledge about humans, human life and human concerns; countless exercises promote personal development, a better life, and professional competences in matters of human life. 90-95% of all humans are archaic humans like people who lived 1000 and 2000 years ago. It is really urgent that you evolve with this book to a very valuable inner status of quality and being.

PSYCHOLOLGY I (ISBN: 1478370661): This book expands the frame of 'Practical Psychology' and presents more precise knowledge about matters of human life and the mind. A lot of practical exercises allow one to reach a high level of genuine personal development. Read rubbish and live with delusions. Remain ignorant. Or take this book in your hands and start becoming a complete and fulfilled human with a precious soul and efficient mind.

POLITICS (ISBN: 1480198714): Politics has failed in

achieving peace on earth, in eliminating the roots of all wars, in creating economic balance, and in promoting human evolution. Outrageous failure! The world needs 10 million and more new politicians and leaders with all-encompassing advanced knowledge and the right personal development. Before you talk about politics and leadership, read this book!

ECONOMICS I (ISBN: 1478226730): The book unveils the dogma and ideology of the biggest scam in modern history that led to the degradation of humanity and the planet via 'profits at all costs'. All business people and those who work in a field of the economy must know what the academic education does not tell you. If you don't want to know, you are a collaborator of the collective destruction.

ECONOMICS II (ISBN: 1478244577): The book delves into the key elements of microeconomics and their intricate relation to financial crises and the omnipresent destructivity exerted on humanity. This book teaches you what you will not learn in accredited economic teaching. Become a robot and servant of the capitalist cynicism or learn about the lies and scams for a new economic world.

ECONOMICS III (ISBN: 1478275626): The book uncovers key facts and figures of the state of humanity and the planet; revealing herewith the systemic failures in economics, politics, education and religion. Not wanting to know about the roots of failures in the economy, in politics, education and religion serves the hidden masters, which systematically destroy the archetypal (genuine) human development. Therefore: Expand your view and serve the human development!

MODERN DREAM THEORY (ISBN: 1478384891): Dreams guide people to the truth, to the power of the inner Spirit. Dream form the ethical, psychological, spiritual and religious foundation of life. Dream shed light on all the principles of the psychical-spiritual growth. Without the 'Spiritual intelligence' of dreams, people can never find fulfillment. There is no better guidance for everyone, regardless of culture, religion or ideology. There is no future for humanity, without taking the power of the inner Spirit seriously.

200 WAYS TO SAVE THE PLANET (ISBN: 1548039209): "Humanity has 25 years left to implement relevant and all-encompassing changes, but must start now." Herein, Dr. Schellhammer outlines 200 concrete ways of practical change for every human being around the globe that can guarantee a change from the cataclysmic roller coaster ride that humanity finds itself on today to a complete renewal in order to bring humanity "back to the path of (archetypal) genuine human evolution," he says.

All books available worldwide on Amazon, in paperback and Kindle version. For German versions, see schellhammerinstitut.com.

SCHELLHAMMER RETREAT

The Schellhammer Retreat is an educational institution that offers a one-of-a-kind Retreat together with a unique self-development educational program. The Schellhammer Retreat is about discovery, spirituality, fulfillment and self-exploration through the process of Individuation. Participants are offered a breakthrough in their personal life, fulfillment in their vocation, a deeper archetypal meaning of life, an inner catharsis, and the complete absolution.

The Schellhammer Retreat is a psychical-spiritual 'Life School' that can lead individuals to high and very high aims of the Individuation Process. It includes the shaping processes of any kind of mission for humanity and the genuine (archetypal) human evolution.

Book yourself a stay: SchellhammerRetreat.com.